I0136649

Stephen Beauregard Weeks

The religious Development in the Province of North Carolina

Stephen Beauregard Weeks

The religious Development in the Province of North Carolina

ISBN/EAN: 9783337130848

Printed in Europe, USA, Canada, Australia, Japan

Cover: Foto ©ninafisch / pixelio.de

More available books at **www.hansebooks.com**

The Religious Development in the Province of North Carolina.

JOHNS HOPKINS UNIVERSITY STUDIES
IN
HISTORICAL AND POLITICAL SCIENCE

HERBERT B. ADAMS, Editor

History is past Politics and Politics present History.—*Freeman*

TENTH SERIES

V–VI

The Religious Development in the Province of North Carolina.

BY STEPHEN BEAUREGARD WEEKS, PH. D.

Professor of History and Political Science, Trinity College, North Carolina.

BALTIMORE
THE JOHNS HOPKINS PRESS
PUBLISHED MONTHLY
May–June, 1892

COPYRIGHT, 1892, BY THE JOHNS HOPKINS PRESS.

THE FRIEDENWALD CO., PRINTERS,
BALTIMORE.

CONTENTS.

CHAPTER I.

INTRODUCTION.

CHAPTER II.

THE STATUS OF RELIGION UNDER THE GRANTS TO THE LORDS PROPRIETORS.

CHAPTER III.

THE FIRST SETTLERS NOT RELIGIOUS REFUGEES.

CHAPTER IV.

THE FIRST STRUGGLE FOR THE ESTABLISHMENT.

CHAPTER V.

THE SECOND STRUGGLE FOR THE ESTABLISHMENT ; ITS RELATIONS TO THE "CARY REBELLION" AND TO THE TUSCARORA WAR.

THE RELIGIOUS DEVELOPMENT IN THE PROVINCE OF NORTH CAROLINA.

CHAPTER I.

INTRODUCTION.

The purpose of this paper is two-fold. In the first place the writer seeks to show that the earliest settlers in North Carolina were not religious refugees; that they came to the province not from religious but mainly from economic motives. In the second place he will trace the progress of the struggle for an Establishment, and will show that, beginning with 1701, the Episcopal Church was for three-quarters of a century the legal church in North Carolina; that, while there was *toleration* for Dissenters, under the rule of this Establishment, there was not, and from necessity could not be, freedom of conscience and soul-liberty in the absolute sense of those terms; that religious freedom, like political freedom, was a growth, and was won only by long and continued struggles.

The writer came to his subject with the belief that the colony had been settled by religious refugees and that there had been absolute freedom of religion. The irresistible logic of facts drove him to his present position. He now believes that the glowing pictures of Mr. Bancroft are overdrawn, and that the self-laudations of native historians in regard to the early religious history of the State are without solid foundation. There was an Established Church; there was positive persecution; there was not religious freedom, and we must acknowledge the facts. The writer believes that, in the light of the documents which have been brought to bear on his subject, his position must be accepted as substantially correct, and that this portion of American history and this chapter in the history of the development of religious freedom must be rewritten.

Religion in all its phases has received but scant attention from most writers on the early history of North Carolina. Following the lead of their predecessors, they assume that in the beginning the colony was settled by religious refugees, that there was always the fullest religious liberty, and that these men and women who are supposed to have fled before the persecuting spirit of other colonies, in the course of a few years lapsed into what Dr. Hawks calls one of the most irreligious communities on the face of the earth. These beliefs and theories are contradictory in themselves. If religious refugees, then how the fullest religious liberty under an Established Church? If refugees, then how could they lapse in the course of a few years into a state but one degree better than barbarism? If the fullest religious liberty and the greatest contentment with the Established Church, then why are the Quakers always the objects of the jealous suspicions and bitter abuse constantly heaped on them by the party of the Church? These are questions which naturally present themselves when the older views are advanced as to the original religious feelings of the colonists. The truth of the matter is that students who have approached the study of our early history have found themselves oppressed by an inability to get at the necessary materials. They have undertaken the task with insufficient resources at their command, and the result has been that their pictures are far from accurate. A careful and scientific study of our history has become possible only within the last few years. With the publication of the Colonial Records of North Carolina, begun in 1886 and finished in 1890, a new storehouse of hitherto unexploited materials has been opened, and it is now possible to get nearer the true state of affairs in the early colony than it has ever been before.

In his first thesis the author will attack a tradition which has become almost sacred to every patriotic citizen of North Carolina. This tradition is that the first settlers of North Carolina were religious refugees, most of them Quakers, fleeing from the persecutions, injuries and insults of the Episcopal Establishment in Virginia and from the bigotry and narrowness of Puritanical New England.

Historians have delighted to represent the province as a home for the weary and oppressed of every sect and nation, as a common refuge for the lovers of soul-liberty the world over. Mr. Bancroft, in his excellent and generally accurate account of the first settlement in North Carolina, closes an eloquent passage by saying that Albemarle, "the child of ecclesiastical oppression, was swathed in independence."[1] Hugh Williamson, whose History of North Carolina was published in 1812, and who has the honor of being the first to undertake such a task after the State became independent, says that the first settlers of the Albemarle colony "were chiefly refugees from ecclesiastical oppression."[2] Martin fol-

---

[1] History of U. S., Vol. II., 136, original edition. In his later editions Mr. Bancroft has modified his statements to a considerable extent.

[2] History of North Carolina, I., 92, note. This is the earliest statement of the claim which I have seen. After quoting extracts from the Virginia laws of 1662 against the Quakers (pp. 81–83), Williamson reasons out their flight to North Carolina after the following fashion: " Many of the most industrious subjects were constrained to leave the colony. They fled to the wilderness, at the distance of eighty or ninety miles from the operation of those laws. Hence it followed, that the first settlers near Pasquetank and Perquimans were chiefly emigrants from Virginia and dissenters from the Established Church of England ; many of them were Quakers." He never deigns to give authorities. Chalmers, with all the blunders of the *Political Annals*, does not give countenance to this. He says the Albemarle colony "being equally destitute of religion and clergy " was "not disturbed like the early colonists of the North with religious controversy." Again, he writes: " Perfect freedom in religion was offered to the people who seem hitherto to have been but little attached to any." Of the law of 1669, providing for civil marriages, he says: "From this remarkable law we may judge of the then state of religion and of morals." It seems clear that this error got its start from Williamson.

lows him in point of time and says, with reference to the year 1660, " The legislature of Virginia having passed laws unfavorable to the Quakers, a number of whom had fled thither from the persecuting spirit of New England, many families sought an asylum on Albemarle Sound." [1]   John H. Wheeler, the next historian of the State, reëchoes this old belief.   He says that North Carolina previous to 1653 had been "the refuge of Quakers, and others fleeing from religious persecutions." [2]   Dr. Hawks, who is by far the most scholarly of our State historians, forgetting for the time his church in his Christianity, says, "The Quakers were no small part of the infant colony: they had fled purposely to escape the tender mercies of the Episcopal establishment in Virginia, and the Puritan model in Massachusetts." [3]   The persecutions endured by the Quakers "sent them into the wilderness of North Carolina, and this persecution began .in New England."   He characterizes this treatment by saying that whether it came from Prelatist or Puritan it was not taught by Christ and was really and truly "damnable wickedness." [4]   The latest historian of the State is John W. Moore, whose work was published in 1880.   He follows the lead of his predecessors, and in speaking of the persecution of Baptists and Quakers in Virginia says, "North Carolina was then beyond the jurisdiction of the petty tyrant who ruled at Williamsburg.   The tender mercies of the Tuscarora seemed preferable to the whippings and brandings practiced in Virginia to prevent nonconformity to the Established Church." [5]

Up to the present time such have been the opinions of the historians in regard to the prime motives in the foundation of the colony of Albemarle from which has grown the State of North Carolina.   As far as the writer knows, not until the last decade has this position been attacked.   In March, 1886, Rev. Joseph Blount Cheshire, Jr., D. D., now of Charlotte, North Carolina, published in the *Church Messenger*

[1] History of North Carolina, I.. 119, 1829.   [2] *Ibid.*, I., 29, 1851.
[3] *Ibid.*, II., 443, 1858. [4] *Ibid.*, II., 361. 362. [5] *Ibid.*, I., 14, Raleigh, 1880.

an article in which he took issue with Bancroft, Hawks and others as to the central motive in the settlement. During the same year Col. Saunders, in his prefatory notes to the first volume of Colonial Records, says, "It is perhaps a very flattering unction that we lay to our souls in supposing our State was settled by men seeking religious freedom, but unhappily there seems to be no solid foundation for the belief." [1] The author of this monograph will undertake to show that the original settlement of North Carolina was due not to religious but mainly to economic reasons.

The second thesis of the author is that religious freedom in North Carolina was a development, just as it was in other States of the American Union. There was an Established Church in North Carolina ; all citizens were required to pay to the support of this Church ; it lasted until swept away by the Revolution, and was considered by many of the inhabitants, as Governor Tryon confesses, even more oppressive than the Stamp Act. The existence of an Establishment has never been given by the historians of the State the prominence which it demands. It is the purpose of this paper to trace the progress of the struggle for the Establishment and to show its relations to other phases of our history. With some of the writers there seems to be a tendency to confuse *toleration* and *liberty of conscience,* and we will find great emphasis laid on the assumed fact of thorough freedom of conscience and of perfect soul-liberty. It is true that there were few persecutions in North Carolina for the sake of religious belief; but for this we have to thank the strength and vigorous policy of the Dissenters rather than any feeling of love and brotherhood among the party of the Established Church. It is usually said that the time has never been when a citizen of North Carolina was not free to worship God after the dictates of his own conscience; but the writer believes that when a Dissenter is forced to pay tithes to support ministers other than his own and when dissent

---

[1] Colonial Records of North Carolina, I., Prefatory Notes, xxi.

carries with it disfranchisement and consequently disgrace, when the Dissenter is shut out from all offices of honor, trust and profit, that there cannot be "freedom of conscience" and "soul-liberty" in the absolute sense.

CHAPTER II.

That portion of the American Continent lying between
31 and 36 degrees, north latitude, was granted on March 24,
1663, by Charles II. to eight of his favorites, who were
among the most wealthy and influential lords of the kingdom.
June 30, 1665, after this vast territory had been somewhat
explored and the Proprietors had learned something of the
position and limits of their new possessions, they secured from
the king a further extension of their charter to 36° 30′ on
the north, which has ever since remained as the northern
boundary of North Carolina, and on the south to 29°. The
grant extended westward to the South Sea. The men honored
by this magnificent donation were Edward Hyde, Earl of
Clarendon; George Monk, Duke of Albemarle; William,
Lord Craven; John, Lord Berkeley; Anthony Ashley Cooper,
Earl of Shaftesbury; Sir George Carteret, Governor of
Jersey; Sir John Colleton; and Sir William Berkeley, Governor of Virginia, the Jeffreys of Bacon's "rebellion," and
the executioner of the first Governor of North Carolina.

Both the charters of Charles II. proceed on the assumption
that the Church of England was to be the Established Church
in the new colony. Toleration of Dissenters was provided
for; but it was not the original purpose of the Proprietors of
Carolina to found a colony with absolute religious freedom,
although the instructions given to their representatives in
America would often lead us to that conclusion. Thus we
find Sir John Colleton writing to the Duke of Albemarle
under the date of June 10, 1663, that the persons designing to
settle in North Carolina "expect liberty of conscience and
without that will not go, which by the patent of Sir Robert

Heath cannot be granted them."[1]   Again, on August 25,
1663, the Proprietors say in their proposals concerning settlements on the Cape Fear, that they "will grant, in as
ample manner as the undertakers shall desire, freedom and
liberty of conscience in all religious or spiritual' things, and
to be kept inviolably with them, we having power in our
charter so to do."[2]   Furthermore, the Proprietors, writing to
Sir William Berkeley, September 8, 1663, in regard to the
appointment of a governor for Albemarle, assign as their
reasons for giving him power to appoint two governors instead
of one in the territory, that " some persons that are for liberty

---

[1] Col. Rec., I., 34. Colleton must here refer to the passage in the charter
of Heath where the king grants him "the patronages and advowsons of
all churches which shall happen to be built hereafter in the said region
. . . to have, exercise, use and enjoy in like manner as any Bishop of
Durham within the Bishopricke or county palatine of Durham." (Col.
Rec., I., 6, 7.)

[2] Col. Rec., I., 45. The first charter of Charles II. reënacts the clause
of Heath's charter which relates to patronages and advowsons. It gives
the Proprietors the power also "to build and found churches, chapels and
oratories . . . and to cause them to be consecrated according to the
ecclesiastical laws of our kingdom of England." (Col. Rec., I., 22.)
Section 18 provides for religious toleration "Because it may happen that
some of the people and inhabitants of the said province, cannot in their
private opinions, conform to the public exercise of religion, according
to the liturgy, form and ceremonies of the church of England, or take
and subscribe the oaths and articles, made and established in that behalf,
and for that the same, by reason of the remote distances of these places,
will, we hope be no breach of the unity and uniformity established in this
nation, our will and our pleasure is and we do . . . give and grant unto
the said Edward, Earl of Clarendon, etc. . . . full and free license, liberty
and authority, . . . to give and grant unto such person or persons . . .
who really in their judgments, and for conscience sake, cannot or shall
not conform to the said liturgy and ceremonies, and take and subscribe
the oaths and articles aforesaid, or any of them, such indulgences and dis-
pensations in that behalf, for and during such time and times, and with
such limitations and restrictions as they . . . shall in their discretion
think fit and reasonable ; and with this express proviso, and limitation
also, that such person and persons . . . shall . . . be subject and obedient
to all other the laws, ordinances, and constitutions of the said province,
in all matters whatsoever as well ecclesiastical as civil." (Col. Rec., I.,
32, 33.)

of conscience may desire a governor of their own proposing."[1]
This power was not exercised, but Dr. Hawks and Mr.
Bancroft, arguing from this fact, from the fact that William
Drummond, the first Governor, happened to be a Scotchman,
and from the erroneous belief that the colony was settled
largely by religious refugees, have assumed that Drummond
was a Presbyterian and that he was appointed because of his
dissenting views; but it is hard to believe that the bigotry of
Sir William Berkeley and the zeal always manifested by the
Proprietors for the Church of England would have allowed
them at any time to appoint a Dissenter to the governorship
because he was a Dissenter.[2]

The terms offered in 1665 to Sir John Yeamans and others,
who were making a settlement on the Cape Fear, bore on
their face the evidence of remarkable liberality. It was
provided that "no person . . . shall be any ways molested,
punished, disquieted or called in question for any differences
in opinion or practice in matters of religious concernment
. . . but that all and every such person and persons may
from time to time and at all times freely and fully have and
enjoy his and their judgments and consciences in matters of
religion throughout all the said province."[3] But this freedom
is limited by the next clause, which gives the Assembly
"power by act to constitute and appoint such and so many
ministers or preachers as they shall think fit, and to
establish their maintenance, giving liberty besides to any
person or persons to keep and maintain what preachers or
ministers they please."[4] Later in the same year we find that
Yeamans, then governor of the Clarendon colony on Cape Fear,
is instructed to do all he can to keep those in the "king's
dominions that either cannot or will not submit to the

---

[1] Col. Rec., I., 54.

[2] The religious faith of Drummond has been discussed by the present
writer in a separate paper on "William Drummond, First Governor of
North Carolina, 1664–1667," in *The National Magazine*, April, 1892.

[3] Col. Rec., I., 80, 81.

[4] *Ibid.*, I., 81.

government of the Church of England."[1]   In 1667 the Proprietors direct Gov. Stephens to see to it that no persons shall be in "any way molested, punished, disquieted or called in question for any differences in opinion or practice in matter of religious concernment who do not actually disturb the civil peace of the said province or county, but that all and every such person and persons may from time to time and at all times freely and fully have and enjoy their judgments and consciences in matter of religion."[2]

In the same way Locke made provisions in his Fundamental Constitutions for the toleration of Dissenters, "that civil peace may be obtained amidst diversity of opinion." He provided that any seven persons agreeing in any religion should be constituted a "church or profession, to which they shall give some name, to distinguish it from others."[3]   Three articles of belief were necessary to constitute any body of persons a church: (1) that there is a God; (2) that God is to be publicly worshipped; (3) that it is lawful and the duty of every man to bear witness to the truth when called on by the proper authority, and "that every church or profession shall in their terms of communion set down the eternal way whereby they witness a truth as in the presence of God."[4]   No man was permitted to be a freeman in Carolina or to have any estate or habitation in it that did not acknowledge a God and that He was to be publicly worshipped.[5]   No person above seventeen years of age could have any benefit or protection of law nor hold any place of profit or honor who was not a member of some church or profession.[6]   No person of one faith was to disturb or molest the religious assemblies of others,[7] nor use reproachful, reviling or abusive language against any church or profession,[8] nor persecute them for speculative opinions in religion or their ways of worship,[9] and every freeman in

---

[1] Col. Rec., I., 94.   [2] *Ibid.*, I., 166.
[3] Fundamental Constitutions, sec. 97.   In Col. Rec., I., pp. 187–207.
[4] Fundamental Constitutions, sec. 100.
[5] *Ibid.*, sec. 95.   [6] *Ibid.*, sec. 101.   [7] *Ibid.*, sec. 102.
[8] *Ibid.*, sec. 106.   [9] *Ibid.*, sec. 109.

Carolina was to have absolute power and authority over his slaves of what opinion or religion soever.[1]

These provisions, while bearing hard on those who had no distinct religious preference, seem liberal enough for those who were earnest and sincere in their religious belief; but such was not the case. In section 96 the doctrine was enunciated that as the country came to be " sufficiently planted and distributed into fit divisions," it should be the duty of " parliament to take care for the building of churches and the public maintenance of divines, to be employed in the exercise of religion according to the Church of England; which being the only true and orthodox, and the national religion of all the king's dominions, is so also of Carolina, and therefore it alone shall be allowed to receive public maintenance by grant of parliament."[2]

These quotations from original sources show clearly enough the animus of the Proprietors in matters religious. They were anxious to have Dissenters settle in and develop their province, but they could never bring themselves to grant these settlers absolute freedom of religion unencumbered by any special rights and privileges to the Church of England, either expressed or implied. They make the fairest and most blandishing promises to would-be settlers. They emphasize what they call " full and free liberty of conscience."[3] But we see that this meant only toleration at best, and toleration is spoken of as something outside of the regular course of· action; as if it were a privilege to be granted or withheld just as the interests of the Proprietors should dictate. They had the wonderful faculty of creating within the same state an

---

[1] Fundamental Constitutions, sec. 110.

. [2] As is well known, Locke was assisted in his work on the Fundamental Constitutions by Shaftesbury, who speaks of "a good and virtuous life, with a hearty endeavor of service to one's country and to mankind, joined with a religious performance of all sacred duties and a conformity with the established rites " as " enough to answer the highest character of Religion." Martin states, History of North Carolina, I., appendix cix., that this section was inserted against the judgment of Locke.

[3] Col. Rec., I., 154, 156.

established church and "full and free liberty of conscience."
It was a generation before the true amount of this " liberty "
began to be seen, and then the hollowness of all their professions was painfully manifest.   That the Proprietors never
intended to divorce the Church and State is indicated by their
frequent grants to Assemblies " to constitute and appoint such
and so many ministers or preachers as they shall think fit,"[1]
by their grants to "each parish" of church sites and a hundred acres of land for the use of the minister,[2] and by the
direct and elaborate provision in the Fundamental Constitutions of Locke; so that in 1670, less than a score of years
after the first settlements were made in the Albemarle country, the colony was dominated by an Established Church, with
a tax upon Dissenters for its support, a religious test for
residence, and church membership demanded before even the
protection of the laws could be claimed.

The question now arises, had Dissenters in England
demanded absolute freedom of religion, even to the abolish-
ing of all tithes, as early as the seventeenth century, or was
this position one of later growth?   This idea was not new.
In the sixteenth century the doctrine had been promulgated
by the Separatists or Brownists, who "rejected the notion of
a National Church, . . . and insisted on the right of each
congregation to perfect independence of faith and worship."[3]

During the reign of Elizabeth they had begun to withdraw
from " attendance at public worship on the ground that the
very existence of a National Church was contrary to the
word of God."[4]   They grew rapidly in numbers; were persecuted alike by the bishops and the Presbyterians, and under
the leadership of John Robinson fled to Holland, where they
developed in freedom their system of independent congregations, each forming a complete church in itself.   To these

---

[1] Col. Rec., I., 167.

[2] *Ibid.*, I., 92.

[3] Green's Short History of English People, Chap. 8, sec. 8.

[4] *Ibid.*, Chap. 8, sec. 1.   *Cf.* also Mr. Paul E. Lauer's paper in the
present series, Chap. 1.

Separatists the name Independents is at a later period attached.

The coming of the Pilgrims to America lessened for the time the prominence of their principles, but they reappear as national questions in the years between the end of the Civil War and the death of the King. "Then for the first time," remarks Green, "began the struggle between political tradition and political progress, between the principle of religious conformity and the principle of religious freedom." In 1646 we find as many as sixteen sects which, although differing among themselves, were all agreed in "repudiating any right of control in faith or worship by the church or its clergy."

The same idea was present in the demands of the New Model of Cromwell, when in June, 1647, they took an oath not to disband until liberty of conscience was secured; and according to their "humble petition," presented to the King in the same month, belief and worship should be free to all. Cromwell was always the true friend of the cause of religious liberty; he became the head of the Independents, and under his rule in 1653 we find a proposal made in Parliament to substitute the free contributions of congregations for the payment of tithes.[1]

In 1633 Roger Williams had opposed the Puritan model of union between Church and State which then obtained in Massachusetts; he was also opposed to all contributions for religious purposes which were not purely voluntary. The whole history of the Quakers, who date from 1644, is one continued protest against the union of Church and State and the payment of tithes.

Absolute separation of Church and State and the abolition of all tithes were not unheard-of demands, then, when the Proprietors provide for an Established Church in Carolina in 1663 and 1669, and when they undertake to make it a reality in 1701 and 1704.

---

[1] Green, Chap. 8, sec. 10.

CHAPTER III.

As we have seen, the claim has been commonly set up that North Carolina was a home for all who were persecuted for conscience sake. This claim has been made in the face of the charters of the King and instructions of the Proprietors. From the excerpts which have been presented it is evident that had religious refugees come to North Carolina after the grant to the Proprietors they could not have found that absolute freedom of religion for which they sought and without which they could not be content; that the germ of an Establishment is to be found in the charters and in the instructions sent their agents by the Proprietors; and that this germ was developed under the Fundamental Constitutions. That no Dissenter could have found religious freedom in North Carolina after 1663 is thus shown from internal evidence; that few came to North Carolina at that time to seek it will be shown by three kinds of external evidence, from the Dissenters themselves, from the Church party, from contemporary and later writers.

The earliest settlers of North Carolina came from Virginia, but the time and method of their coming are shrouded in uncertainty. We find that in 1653 the legislature of Virginia, in response to a petition from Roger Green, "clarke," "on behalf of himself and inhabitants of Nansemond River," made to him a personal grant of 1000 acres and a communal grant of 10,000 acres for a colony of a hundred persons who were to go from Virginia and settle in the present county of Bertie in North Carolina. This is usually pointed to as the first of these southward migrations for conscience sake; but Green is styled " clarke," that is, minister, by the Virginia statute. This term was applied in the laws only to clergymen of the Established Church, and his title disproves then, at once, all claims that in removing to Carolina Green was seeking greater liberty. We are not quite sure that this proposed movement was ever carried into effect,[1] but that colonists soon began to come down into the Albemarle section of North Carolina and that a number of families were settled there before 1660 is quite certain.

In March, 1662, Kilcacenen, King of the Yeopim Indians, sold a tract of land to George Durant in the section still known as Durant's Neck; this tract lay beside another tract which the king had "formerly sold to Samuel Pricklove."[2] The next year George Catchmany came forward with a claim for the whole section which he held under a prior grant from the Governor of Virginia.[3] There were also other direct purchases from the Indians, for as early as 1662 these had become such an evil that the government of Virginia was resolved to tolerate them no longer. Other persons besides Catchmany held grants also from the Governor of Virginia, and in section four of the first charter of Charles II. to the Proprietors we find a saving clause inserted evidently for their relief: "and saving also the right, title and interest of all and every our subjects of the English nation, which are now planted within the limits and bounds aforesaid (if any be)."

As to the religious inclinations of these earliest colonists nothing is known absolutely. All the indirect testimony tends to establish the belief that they had been reared within the pale of the English Church and sympathized with it as far as they had any religious preference; but as there was no Christian ministry among them, this sympathy and preference gradually waned. The Proprietors had made full provisions for the payment of quit-rents; they had established a church theoretically; they had failed utterly in all practical provi-

---

[1] Colonial Records, I., Prefatory Notes, xxi.
[2] *Ibid.*, I., 19.
[3] *Ibid.*, I., 20.

sions for the souls of men, for the act passed October 15, 1669,[1] to provide for civil marriages, recites "that there is no minister as yet in this county" [country], and we may presume that had even a Dissenter been then living in North Carolina, he might have been allowed to perform the ceremony of marriage as a *dernier ressort.*

The first minister of Christ to preach in North Carolina was William Edmundson, a Quaker, and a native of Westmoreland, England. He was a man of rude eloquence, of earnest piety and shrewd common sense. He showed unusual self-denial, and was charitable to a fault. In a study of the religious history of North Carolina he deserves more than a passing mention, for it is on his foundation that we have been building for two hundred years. Edmundson was born in 1627, and was apprenticed to a carpenter in York. As soon as his apprenticeship was over he joined the Parliamentary army and accompanied Cromwell to Scotland in 1650. He took part the next year in the battle of Worcester and the siege of the Isle of Man. In 1652 he was engaged in recruiting for the Scotch army. A little later he married and settled in Antrim, Ireland, and opened a shop there. During a visit to England in 1653 he again met with the Quakers and embraced their creed. He began to preach and suffered numerous persecutions and imprisonments. From 1661 he was recognized as the leader of the Quakers in Ireland, and his house became practically the headquarters of the Society. In 1665 he was excommunicated for not paying tithes, and suffered more persecutions. He visited America in 1671, and North Carolina in the spring of 1672.[2] He has preserved an account of this visit in his journal, and this account, both by direct and indirect testimony, shows most clearly that the author did not come into a Quaker settlement, and his

---

[1] Col. Rec., I., 184.

[2] Edmundson's visit to North Carolina is mentioned in his journal under the years 1671-72, no exact date being given. Janney, in his History of the Friends (II., 252, 1867), says that Fox and Edmundson were in Maryland in April, 1672, and thence Edmundson journeyed toward the south.

success in making converts is in itself an indisputable proof
that he was not going among religious refugees of other
creeds. Edmundson on his visit to North Carolina encount-
ered many natural obstacles, and tells most graphically of a
night spent in the primitive forest. "It being dark, and the
woods thick, I walked all night between two trees; and
though very weary, I durst not lie down on the ground, for
my clothes were wet to my skin. I had eaten little or nothing
that day, neither had I anything to refresh me but the Lord."[1]
In the morning he and his two companions reached the house
of Henry Phillips, situate on "Albemarle" (Perquimans)
river, where the town of Hertford now stands.[2] Phillips
"and his wife had been convinced of the truth in New England, and came here to live; and not having seen a Friend
for seven years before, they wept for joy to see us."[3] Edmundson and his companions reached the house of Phillips on Sun-
day morning and desired him to appoint a meeting for about
noon of the same day. Many people attended the services,
"but they had little or no religion, for they came and sat
down in the meeting smoking their pipes." But the power
of God was there; some of their hearts were softened and
they "received the testimony." One Tems [Toms], a justice
of the peace, and his wife were among the converts. They
desired the preacher to hold a meeting at their house, which
was about three miles off and "on the other side of the water."
A meeting was held there the next day, and with success,
"for several were tendered with a sense of the power of God,
received the truth and abode in it." Edmundson left North
Carolina on Tuesday of the same week and returned to
Virginia.

---

[1] Edmundson, Journal, 67 (edition 1774). The passages relating to
North Carolina are reprinted in the Col. Rec., I., 215 *et seq.*

[2] Moore, History of North Carolina, I., 20.

[3] The belief of Martin in the refugee theory is so strong that he changes
this statement of Edmundson into "not having seen any leader of this
society." He also inaccurately gives the name of the Quaker as Phelps
instead of Phillips (I., 155).

George Fox was the second missionary to visit North Carolina. He entered the colony with three companions, Robert Widders, James Lancaster and George Pattison, on November 21, 1672, *via* Somerton, Virginia, and went by canoe down Bennett's creek, called by him Bonner's creek, into the Chowan river, to the house of Hugh Smith, " where people of other professions came to see us (no Friends inhabiting that part of the country)." This house was probably situate in the western part of the present county of Chowan, and from it Fox and his companions passed by water to the house of the Governor, which seems to have been where the town of Edenton now is. The Governor and his wife received them "lovingly," but they found a skeptic in the person of a certain doctor who "would needs dispute with us," declaring that the light and the Spirit of God were not in the Indians, and who "ran out so far that at length he would not own the Scriptures." From here they visited Perquimans and Pasquotank. At the house of Joseph Scott, a representative of the county, they had "a sound precious meeting ; the people were tender, and much desired after meetings." About four miles further on they had another meeting, to which came the chief secretary of the province, who "had been formerly convinced," due no doubt to the preaching of Edmundson. "Having visited the north part of Carolina, and made a little entrance for the truth among the people there, we began to return again towards Virginia, having several meetings in our way, wherein we had good service for the Lord, the people being generally tender and open. . . In our return we had a very precious meeting at Hugh Smith's . . . the people were very tender, and very good service we had amongst them. . . . The ninth of the tenth month we got back to Bonner's creek. . . having spent about eighteen days in north of Carolina."[1]

---

[1] Fox, Journal, 458, 459. Parts relating to North Carolina reprinted in Colonial Records, I., 216–218. Dr. Hawks, who wrongly interprets the "ninth month " of the Quaker to mean September, has blended the separate visits of Fox and Edmundson into one and says that they descended the Roanoke river instead of the Chowan. It is evident that he had never

Edmundson made a second visit to North Carolina in 1676.
He seems to have gone over nearly the same route as in 1672,
but the difference in the forms of expression in his journal is
significant.   It is no longer the preacher who appoints the
meetings, but we find that "they," the members, say when
and where they should be held, indicating that the Society
of Friends was now on a sure footing in North Carolina, and
not unorganized and non-existent as it had been in 1672.
Edmundson held a meeting at the home of his old friend
Toms, and says in concluding : "I had several precious meetings in that colony, and several turned to the Lord.   People
were tender and loving, and there was no room for the priests,
for Friends were finely settled and I left things well among
them." [1]

The Friends were the first to send missionaries into
the wilds of Carolina.   These missionaries were William
Edmundson and George Fox.   What conclusions may we
draw from the journals of Edmundson and Fox in regard to
the state of religion in the early days of the colony and in
regard to religious denominations there at that time?   In
the first place, besides the case of Phillips, the author has
been able to find no other example in the early history of the
colony that suggests, or can be so construed as to indicate,
persecution as a motive for settlement.   The statement that
Phillips and his wife had not seen a Friend in seven years
indicates clearly that there were none in that part of Carolina,
at least.   Seven years carries us back to 1665, when there
were probably about 500 families in the settlement.[2]   Is it
probable that a Quaker would have lived for seven years in

seen Edmundson's Journal, and his reading of Fox's Journal, to which he
refers, must have been very careless for him to make such a blunder as
this (History of North Carolina, II., 363), especially when Fox says himself that when he and his companions returned to Maryland, from
" Friends we understood that William Edmundson having been at Rhode
Island and New England was returned to Ireland " (Journal, 461).

[1] Journal, 112–115, reprinted in Col. Rec., I., 226, 227.
[2] Oldmixon gives 300 families in 1663.

a place where his brethren were all around him without once visiting them and exhorting them to good works? and this, too, where the whole area of the settlement was not more than forty miles square, his home near the center, and all points accessible by water? Few things could have been more improbable.

In the second place, the accounts do not indicate that the settlers were men of fixed views in matters of creed. Had they been Quakers they would no doubt have had regular times and places for worship, as their services are very simple; they do not recognize the ministry as a separate calling, and every member of the body of Friends is at liberty to conduct religious meetings when moved by the Spirit; moreover, instead of having the meeting appointed by the visiting brother, they would have perhaps done this themselves had there been an organized society, as they did at the time of Edmundson's second visit in 1676. If these settlers were persecuted Baptists or Presbyterians we cannot explain their easy conversion to a new form of faith. Only men and women of strong character and fixed belief become religious exiles; nor would such men in less than a score of years have given up the faith of their fathers, for which they had exiled themselves from civilized society, and adopted a new and untried form of belief. Their indulgence in the pipe, while evidently done with no purpose to disturb the worship, shows very clearly their ignorance of its forms and ceremonies and that they, like Henry Phillips, had seen neither a Friend nor any other minister in seven years and more. They had forgotten how to conduct themselves on such occasions, for the simple truth of the matter is that these were the first religious meetings ever held in Carolina. The men who attended them were not habitual lawbreakers and outcasts from the moral universe. They had settled in this wilderness for political and economic reasons or to gratify that love of adventure and travel so characteristic of the Teutonic race. Fox found a people who realized their need of religion. They were "tender and open," he says, and many of them no doubt, in the solitude of an unexploited wilderness and in the midst of the dangers and hardships attendant on a new order of things, had felt the sweet and strengthening influence of that power which comes from above. They were religious; but they had no bigotry; many of them perhaps did not fancy the outward appearance and form of Quakerism; but they felt the need of religious organization; they saw that nothing was to be expected from the Proprietors; for they had done nothing beyond the theoretical establishment of a church and had then abandoned the colony in a way that was thoroughly characteristic of all their actions when their pecuniary interests were not at stake. The colonists had been left to grope after spiritual things without help from man, and the episode of the pipes indicates that many had fallen short of what are called the proprieties of life; but their hearts were right, and when the grace of God is offered them in their own homes they accept it with gladness and a vigorous branch of the Christian Church is founded. The true beginnings of the Quaker element in North Carolina are to be found in converts made on her soil, and not in immigrants fleeing from religious persecution in New England and Virginia.

No argument in favor of the refugee theory can be based, then, on the journals of Edmundson and Fox. They tell us in substance that they found no Quakers during their first visit, and the whole tone of their journals is against it. To this negative testimony we have the direct and positive testimony of the party of the Established Church. Henderson Walker, then Governor, writing to the Bishop of London under date of October 21, 1703, states clearly that the first settlers were not Quakers. He says: "We have been settled near this fifty years in this place, and I may justly say most part of twenty-one years, on my own knowledge, without priest or altar, and before that time, according to all that appears to me, much worse. George Fox, some years ago, came into these parts, and, by strange infatuations, did infuse the Quaker's principles into some small number of the people; which did and hath continued to grow ever since very numerous, by reason of their yearly sending in men to encourage and exhort them to their wicked principles; and here was none to dispute nor to oppose them in carrying on their pernicious principles for many years."[1] William Gordon, writing to the Secretary of the Society for the Propagation of the Gospel on May 13, 1709, says: "There are few or no dissenters in this government but Quakers, who . . . . plead that they were the *first* settlers . . . . but this (according to the best accounts I could get) seems false in fact,—that religion being scarce heard of there till some years after the settlement; it is true some of the most ancient inhabitants, after George Fox went over, did turn Quakers."[2]

What then was the leading motive in the settlement of Carolina? Why did Englishmen come from the Bermudas, from Virginia and from New England to settle amid the unexploited wilds of Carolina? Was it merely to gratify a spirit of adventure, to satisfy the longings for new and untried scenes, or was there a deeper and more material motive in this movement?

The desire for more land and better land was one of the leading factors, if not the chief one, in the settlement of North Carolina. The Anglo-Saxon has ever been noted for his love for the ownership of land. The mother-country was crowded. He came to Virginia and New England. Virginia increased in population, New England was barren, and the colonist in every age has loved wide and fertile fields. This explains the present rush to the Northwest; this explains the incredible growth of Oklahoma. In the seventeenth century, as now, the colonist was ever eager for a wide stretch of bottom land. "Up stream and up creek, across divides to other water courses, there was ever the same object in view, more bottom land and better bottom land."[3]

---

[1] Col. Rec., I., 571.   [2] *Ibid.*, I., 708, 710.
[3] Col. Saunders in Prefatory Notes to Col. Rec., I., xxi.

The soil of northeastern North Carolina, moreover, had few equals on the globe. It was level, well wooded, and so fertile that if the surface was but scratched it brought forth heavy returns. Its natural products were so varied and bountiful that both man and beast found a large part of their sustenance ready prepared in nature's storehouse. The broad and navigable rivers furnished easy means of communication and were well stocked with excellent fish. The Indians were peaceable, and there were few extremes in temperature. In no country was a living gained with less labor than in Carolina. The settlers were agriculturists and took up large tracts of territory. They lived miles perhaps from their neighbors. They were surrounded by their families and slaves; they produced all things needed for home consumption; they lived in economic independence if not in elegance, and were content so long as imbecile Governors and ignorant Proprietors left the affairs of the colony in their own hands.

Besides the natural attractions to be found in the climate and soil of Carolina we have contemporary evidence that land, and not religious freedom, was the object of the earliest settlers. Nor do all later writers give countenance to the refugee theory. Janney, who makes copious use of the journals of the fathers of the Society of Friends for his *History of Friends,* makes no claim that there were Quakers in North Carolina prior to the coming of Edmundson and Fox in 1672.[1] Bowden, in his *History of the Society of Friends in America,* does not claim any of the earliest settlers as Quakers with the exception of Phillips. He even states that "there appears not to have been a religious sect in the colony."[2] This egregious claim seems to have been set up for the first time by Williamson, on what authority we are at a loss to say. It is not countenanced by the earlier writers on the province. Governor Johnston wrote to the Board of Trade in 1749 that "the province of North Carolina was first settled by people from Virginia in low circumstances

---

[1] II., pp. 258, 262, 263.   [2] I., 409, 411.

who moved hither for the benefit of a larger and better range for their stocks." [1]

The account of John Lawson gives no support to the refugee theory. This account was written about 1708, and the author was near enough to the founders of the commonwealth to know their real motives for settlement. This was made not for religious but for economic reasons, "by several substantial planters from Virginia and other plantations; who finding mild winters, and a fertile soil beyond expectations, producing everything that was planted to a prodigious increase; their cattle, horses, sheep and swine, breeding very fast, and passing the winter without any assistance from the planter; so that everything seemed to come by nature, the husbandman living almost void of care, and free from those fatigues which are absolutely requisite in winter countries, for providing fodder and other necessaries; these encouragements induced them to stand their ground, although but a handful of people, seated at a great distance one from another, . . . the fame of this new discovered summer country spread through the neighboring colonies, and in a few years drew a considerable number of families thereto." [2]

But if this accumulation of evidence is insufficient to convince any one, we have clear and distinct testimony to the same effect from a contemporary, who was a resident of the colony, a member of the Governor's council, and a man whose business as surveyor-general would give him a better opportunity to discover the motives of the settlers than any other profession. This man was Thomas Woodward. He writes under the date of June 2, 1665, to Sir John Colleton and advises him for the present not to allow settlers to seat themselves beyond certain prescribed limits, and in the next place warns him that "The proportion of land you have allotted with the rent, and condition are by most people not well resented [received] and the very rumor of them dis-

[1] Col. Rec., IV., 920.
[2] History of Carolina, pp. 109, 110, edition 1860.

courages many who had intentions to have removed from Virginia hither : Whilst my lord Baltimore allowed to every person imported but fifty acres, Maryland for many years had scarce fifty families . . . but when he allowed one hundred acres for a person, it soon began to people . . . so if your Lordships pleased to give large encouragement for some time till the country is more fully peopled, your honour may contract for the future upon what condition you please, but for the present, to think that any men will remove from Virginia upon harder conditions than they can live there will prove (I fear) a vain imagination, it being land· only that they come for." [1]

---

[1] Col. Rec., I., 100.

CHAPTER IV.

THE FIRST STRUGGLE FOR THE ESTABLISHMENT.

The last quarter of the seventeenth century was the golden age of Quakerism in North Carolina. The Friends were the first, of "all who profess and call themselves Christians," to labor in this new field. During this period they met with no rivals. No other dissenting ministers appeared in the colony. The Church of England, provided for so elaborately by the Fundamental Constitutions of Locke, had been developed in theory only; no Episcopal ministers had come to the colony; no parishes had been laid off, no churches had been built, no tithes had been levied; absolutely nothing was done by the Established Church for the spiritual advancement of North Carolina prior to 1700; and when the eighteenth century dawned, the Quakers, by their thorough organization, by their earnest preaching, by their simple and devoted lives, by their faithfulness and love, had gathered into their fold many men and women who belonged primarily to other denominations, and who might have remained there had any other opportunity for worship been granted them. But this privilege was denied; they became Friends and remained faithful to their new-found form of belief.

The Society of Friends was thoroughly organized as early as 1676. In 1681 Fox advised them to unite with Friends in South Carolina in establishing a yearly or half-yearly meeting.[1] In 1689 a quarterly meeting was begun, and prior to 1690 their manuscript records show that Quakers were coming into the province from Pennsylvania and Ireland. They had no meeting-houses prior to 1703, but traveling Friends visited them from time to time and had "many comfortable meetings." They begin to appear as a promi-

---

[1] Bowden, I., 413.

nent political factor after the appointment of John Archdale
as Governor of Carolina in 1694. Archdale was a convert
of Fox and had been in North Carolina as early as 1683,
representing the interests of his father, who was a Proprietor.
He visited the colony again in 1686 and administered affairs
during the temporary absence of Sothel. He was in North
Carolina a third time soon after his elevation to the governorship, and in the fall of 1694 appointed Thomas Harvey
deputy governor. Harvey ruled the colony with satisfaction
to all parties. The good work inaugurated by Archdale was
continued; the colonists enjoyed peace within and without;
their general progress was steadily upward; but the golden
age was drawing to its close.

Archdale had been sagacious, prudent and moderate. His
arrival was like balm to the colony, long torn and bleeding
from political dissensions and from the misrule of ignorant
Proprietors and villainous Governors. These troubles were
ended by his coming. The colonists set themselves at once to
recover lost vantage-ground, and seem to have entered on a
period of prosperity and quiet which had hitherto never been
known in their troublesome history. Archdale's faith tended
also to encourage religion and morality. The Quakers
received an impetus which gave them the prestige and power
needed to carry them through the struggles of the next
twenty years. While enforcing a military law Archdale
exempted all Friends from service, and they now began to
appear more frequently than formerly as holders of office.
The Council, the Courts and the Assembly soon showed a
preponderance of Quaker influence. There was a material
reward for being a Quaker, and Churchmen and others who
thus found it to their interests deserted their own creeds to
enroll themselves among the Friends.[1]

There were, however, many men and women in the colony
who remained faithful under all disadvantages to the tradi-
tions and usages of the English Church and who led pious

---

[1] Col. Rec., I., 708; Hawks, II., 364.

and godly lives. It is certain that the Churchmen, together
with those who professed little or no religion, were numerically the stronger. There is no evidence to show that the
Quakers were ever in the majority, but they had the virtual
control of affairs from the appointment of Archdale to the
governor-generalship in 1694 until the death of Deputy
Governor Thomas Harvey on July 3, 1699.

Up to this time there seems to have been no law in the
colony against Dissenters. There may have been a few cases
where Quakers were imprisoned for not bearing arms, as was
the case in 1680,[1] but this instance seems to have been a
political rather than a religious affair; and as their records
are almost entirely silent on this point, we may assume that
they enjoyed perfect religious freedom, except so far as the
knowledge that the Church of England was in theory the
established church of the land might oppress them.

But things were to change. On the death of Harvey,
Henderson Walker became deputy governor, not under any
appointment from the Proprietors, but in virtue of his office as
president of the Council.[2] Walker was born in 1660, perhaps
in Virginia. He migrated to the colony of Albemarle when
just arriving at manhood, and by ability and energy rose to
the highest office in the colony. He was a zealous Churchman,
and during his rule saw the first minister of the Church of
England established in North Carolina. This clergyman was,
the Rev. Daniel Brett. He came out in 1700, and seems to
have been sent by the Society for Promoting Christian Knowledge, whose founder and guiding spirit was the Rev. Thomas
Bray. Brett brought with him a small library given by the
Society, and the first one for public use in North Carolina.[3]

---

[1] MS. Records of Perquimans Monthly Meeting.
[2] Col. Rec., I., 530.
[3] *Ibid.*, I., 572. Walker here says that the library was given by "the
honourable the corporation for the Establishing the Christian Religion,"
which was all no doubt intended to mean the S. P. C. K. Aug. 5, 1701,
a letter "from the Rev. Mr. Daniell Brett of North Carolina to Dr. Bray"
was read before that Society, and this indicates that Brett came out under
its directions. *Cf.* Rev. Edmund McClure's "A Chapter in English
Church History, Journal of the S. P. C. K.," p. 143.

From the glimpse we have of Brett's career we may conclude that he entered his profession not from any sense of duty but simply as a means of support. The few lines devoted to him in Henderson Walker's letter to the Bishop of London on Oct. 21, 1703, are painful in the extreme and show that he was an unfortunate person to be intrusted with the direction of the legal church of the land. Gov. Walker says: "He for about half a year behaved himself in a modest manner, but after that in a most horrid manner, broke out in such an extravagant course that I am ashamed to express his carriage, it being so high a nature. It hath been a great trouble and grief to us who have a great veneration for the Church, that the first minister who was sent us should prove so ill as to give the dissenters so much occasion to charge us with him."[1] Thus ended in shame and disgrace the first missionary effort made by the Church of England to preach the Gospel in North Carolina. Its first clergyman flashes before our eyes like a meteor, as transient and as uncertain. His fall gave scoffers an opportunity to deride and strengthened the cause of the Dissenters. His coming was productive only of harm. We know nothing and care nothing for his fate. From the known purity of Dr. Bray we must believe that he was entirely ignorant of this fellow's character; but he was most unfortunate in his selections, for Brett is only a prototype of Urmstone, Blacknall, Boyd and Moir.

The writer does not believe that the presence of Brett hastened materially the Act of 1701. While his presence would tend to unite the scattered followers of the English Church, his subsequent evil conduct tended materially, on the other hand, to disorganize and divide them. What they had been waiting and watching for was the strong arm of a leader who could unite and concentrate their scattered forces. This man appears in the person of Henderson Walker. He represents a rebound from the Quaker rule of the former years. He stands for the idea of authority as opposed to the individual-

---

[1]Col. Rec., I., 572.

ism and democratic tendencies of Fox and his followers. Under his guiding hand the Churchmen ride into power.

In the autumn of 1701, the Churchmen, by "a great deal of care and management," secured an Assembly which passed an act making the Church of England the Established Church of the colony. Under this law parishes were laid out, the erection of churches was provided for, and a maintenance of £30 was promised to each minister. To meet these expenses a poll tax was levied on every tithable person, and the collectors were given power to distrain in case of refusal. The act was, in accord with the requirements, submitted to the Proprietors for their approval.[1]

But the zealous Churchmen could not endure the delay that must follow reporting the act to the Proprietors and began work at once under its provisions. December 15, 1701, the vestry of Chowan precinct, which had been appointed "in obedience to an act of Assembly made November 12th," and which seems to have been the first Episcopal organization in the province, met at the house of Thomas Gillam and made arrangements for the erection of a house of worship. They elected Col. William Wilkinson and Capt. Thomas Leuten churchwardens, and instructed them to agree with a workman in regard to building a church, twenty-five feet long, "posts in the ground and held to the collar beams."[2] The builder was John Porter, who received £25 for his work.[3] It was finished prior to October 13, 1702, but did not give satisfaction at first because the vestry believed that the boards were not "fit for ceiling such a house."[4] It was accepted on December 15 on condition that Porter "provide so much lime as will wash the ceiling of the chapel."[5] This was the first house of worship erected in North Carolina. Its location cannot be definitely fixed. Dr. Hawks thinks that it was in

---

[1] Col. Rec., I., 544, 572; Hawks, II., 357. The original act has not been preserved.

[2] Col. Rec., I., 544.   [3] *Ibid.*, I., 559.

[4] *Ibid.*, I., 560.   [5] *Ibid.*, I., 561.

or near Edenton, and he is doubtless correct.[1] When com-
pleted it was served by Richard Curton as reader. He
received £7 10s. for his services, but a year later had dis-
appeared. In 1703 two other houses were being erected. The
law directed that the churchwardens should provide weights
and measures for the use of the precinct, together with " one
fair and large book of common prayer, and the book of
homilies."[2] The wardens sent a special messenger to Williamsburg for the three church Bibles intended for the
province, and to each of these three churches Gov. Francis
Nicholson, of Virginia, " of his pious goodness," gave £10.

The legislative act of 1701 had not been carried without
"a great deal of care and management," as Walker confesses.
It had aroused, moreover, the spirit of all the Dissenters.
Those opposed to the Church by reason of the taxes imposed
joined the Quakers, who opposed it on principle ; a vigorous
campaign was carried on, and the anti-Church party returned
a majority of their nominees to the Assembly of 1703. " My
Lord," writes Walker to the Bishop of London in October,
1703, " I humbly beg leave to inform you, that we have
an Assembly to sit the 3d November next, above one half
of the burgesses chosen are Quakers, and have declared
their designs of making void the act for establishing the
Church; if your lordship, out of your good and pious care
for us, doth not put a stop to their growth, we shall the most
part, especially the children born here, become heathens."[3]

The question of an Established Church in North Carolina
had been thus squarely precipitated. The party in favor of
its establishment had thrown down the gauntlet to the Dissenters, and the latter had not been slow in accepting the
challenge. They announced their intention of repealing the
law of 1701, but were spared this trouble by the Proprietors,
who returned the bill disallowed on the ground that £30 was

---

[1] Hawks, II., 341.
[2] Col. Rec., I., 558.
[3] *Ibid.*, I., 572.

an insufficient allowance for the support of a clergyman.[1] The Establishment had gained three churches under the act ; it could expect nothing more.

Thus ends the first act in the great struggle to divorce the State and Church. Thanks to the Proprietors, matters had not yet come to the worst. The Separatists had been success-ful, but they were not allowed to rest on their laurels. They soon learned that eternal vigilance was to be the price of their religious liberty, and they seemed never disinclined to pay it. Their opposition could be carried on more successfully under the leadership of the Quakers because of the thorough organ-ization of that Society into monthly and yearly meetings, which made them like an iron wedge in the midst of yielding wood. They were stable in the midst of instability. They were the Jacobins of the pending revolution.

---

[1] Col. Rec., I., 601. On the sufficiency of this allowance compare Gold-smith's famous line,

"And passing rich with forty pounds a year."

Compare also Mill, Political Economy, Bk. II., ch. xiv., sec. 3. By the 12th of Queen Anne it is declared "That whereas for want of sufficient maintenance and encouragement to curates, the cures have in several places been meanly supplied, the Bishop is therefore empowered to appoint by writing under his hand and seal a sufficient certain stipend or allow-ance, not exceeding fifty, and not less than twenty pounds a year." Adam Smith says that in his day, notwithstanding this provision, forty pounds a year was reckoned very good pay for a curate, and there were many curacies under twenty pounds a year. Lecky, quoting Burnet, in his History of England in the Eighteenth Century, bears witness to this state of affairs, and shows that the condition of the ordinary pastor was so poor at that time that the common artisan would hardly exchange places with him. In rejecting this act the Proprietors were demanding more of the colonists for their clergy than was given to the same class of men in England.

CHAPTER V.

The first attempt to fix the Church of England on the colony of North Carolina as the state religion was internal in its origin. It was precipitated by the General Assembly, and was the crystallization of the wishes and desires of a very large and respectable part of the colonists themselves. It represented their spontaneous effort to return to the order of things to which they had been accustomed in their former homes in Virginia and England. As the first struggle for the Establishment came from within, so the second struggle came from without, and was more reprehensible than the first in proportion as external influence was brought to bear in fixing the Church of England as the State Church upon a large body of Dissenters who had demanded freedom of religion before settling in the province. These Dissenters seem to have regarded the Church as provided for in the charter of the Proprietors as a theory merely, never likely to be realized as a condition ; and it soon became apparent that the exhaustive provisions of the Fundamental Constitutions could never be executed in a country as free as Carolina. Up to the time when the Act of 1701 was passed North Carolina had enjoyed practically absolute freedom of conscience although theoretically under an Establishment. The effort to realize this theory threw all the Dissenters into a single compact body of opponents. This body was composed of Scotch Presbyterians, Dutch Lutherans, French Calvinists, Irish Catholics and American Quakers.[1] It was not the tax, paltry in itself, against which these men were fighting, it

---

[1] Martin, History of North Carolina, I., 218.

was the principle involved.   The power to tax implies
the power to destroy, and, if the Dissenters were to admit this
authority, the liberty which they had enjoyed for a quarter
of a century was at an end.   It was not the amount of the
ship-money that led to the great English rebellion, nor was
it the amount of the taxes imposed that prepared the way for
the American rebellion in 1775; but in each case it was
principle.   Men fight less for material facts than they do for
moral principles.   In this struggle in North Carolina
against spiritual power and usurpation, those who contended
for the ethical idea were readily joined by the mob, who,
always godless, cared more for the tithes than for the principles of freedom, and by a few men like Edward Moseley,
who were themselves devoted Churchmen, but who, like
Patrick Henry and Thomas Jefferson toward the close of the
century, took their position against the Establishment because
it was right.

The attempted enforcement of the Act of 1701 and the
struggle against it do not seem to have caused any serious
disturbance; for while Walker was a Churchman, he was also
a citizen of the colony.   He desired to see it prosper, and we
can readily believe that he did all he could, consistently with
his position as a steady supporter of the Establishment, to
allay the domestic broils and internal disorders.   Compared
with what was to come, his administration did give to the
colony "that tranquillity which it is to be wished it may
never want," as his tombstone makes claim;[1] but he died on
April 14, 1704, and it was left to his successors to set the
two factions in the colony in arms against each other, to
exhaust its internal resources and thus invite the bloody
onslaught of the Tuscaroras in 1711.

From the appointment of Archdale to the governor-
generalship in 1694, the Proprietors seem to have practically
abandoned the colony to its own resources.   During the first
five of these years it had been presided over by an appointee

---

[1] Wheeler, History of North Carolina, I., 34.

of the Governor-General, a man thoroughly versed in their affairs and in full sympathy with them. Their ruler during the last five had been chosen by themselves. The colony had flourished under the control of Harvey and Walker, but this state of things was now to be changed.

The Proprietors had commissioned Sir Nathaniel Johnson Governor-General of the Carolinas in 1702. After the death of Walker he was instructed to appoint a deputy governor for North Carolina. He appointed Col. Robert Daniel, who had been a resident of South Carolina for some years. He had distinguished himself at a recent attack on St. Augustine. He was a Landgrave under the Fundamental Constitutions. He was cruel and merciless in disposition, but had great zeal for the Established Church.

The Church party also received strength from the newly organized Society for the Propagation of the Gospel in Foreign Parts. This Society was the work of Rev. Thomas Bray, who arrived in America in 1700 to examine the religious needs of the colonists. It is probable that he visited North Carolina, and on his return to England recommended that two missionaries be sent to that province, whose Governor "being a very worthy gentleman, I dare promise will give the best countenance and encouragement which shall be in his power."[1]

---

[1] Hawks, II., 339. Bray's report was printed in 1700 after his return. Stephen (Dict. National Biog., Art. Bray) makes no mention of a visit to America earlier than the one begun December 16, 1699. It seems then that Dr. Hawks is in error when he says that Bray "remained in America two or three years"(Hist., II., 338). In 1701 Dr. Bray published a memorial "representing the present state of religion in the several provinces on the Continent of North America, in order to the providing a sufficient number of missionaries so absolutely necessary to be sent at this juncture into those parts," folio, London. It is republished in the Prot. Epis. Hist. Soc. Coll., pp. 99–106. From this memorial it appears that outside of Virginia and Maryland there were not half a dozen clergymen in all the colonies, and that including these two colonies there were hardly forty in all. North Carolina was not so much worse off than her neighbors, then. *Cf.* Perry, Hist. Amer. Epis. Church, I., 203.

The first representative of the Society in North Carolina was Rev. John Blair, who came out in January, 1704. He found the people scattered, the means of communication poor, the Dissenters strong and the Churchmen lukewarm. The Assembly of 1704 did nothing toward settling his maintenance; he became discouraged and left the colony in a few months. His mission was an utter failure. He has given us the reasons for it. There was a lack of inhabitants to maintain the ministers; the territory was entirely too large for one man to serve. Blair says that he was one hundred and twenty miles from any other clergyman and that he traveled thirty miles a day, Sundays excepted. The precincts were each bounded by two rivers. These rivers were about twenty miles apart and there were no settlers in the interior. The new colony of Pamlico, moreover, lay far to the south, separated from the others by a "pond five miles broad."[1] Under these circumstances it will be seen that only failure could await the missionary. Besides these physical disadvantages, the Society had to struggle against indifference at home to mission work[2] and an active body of Dissenters in the colony. Dr. Blair divides the inhabitants of Albemarle into four classes according to their religious affiliations: (1) the Quakers, who were "the most powerful enemies to Church government, but a people very ignorant of what they profess"; (2) those who have no religion, but would be Quakers if it did not demand greater purity of life; (3) the third sort are something like Presbyterians, "upheld by some idle fellows who have left their lawful employment, and preach and baptize through the country without any manner of orders from any sect or pretended church"; (4) zealous Churchmen, fewest in number, "but the better sort of people." The first three classes were all of different pretensions, but they made common cause "to prevent anything that will be chargeable to

[1] Col. Rec., I., 600 *et seq.*
[2] *Cf. ibid.*, I., 604, for the petition of the people of Bath county to Parliament for a minister. It seems not to have been noticed.

them, as they allege church government will be, if once established by law."[1]

The mission of Dr. Blair was not without its effect on the future religious development of North Carolina, however. It served to bring out fairly and squarely the religious politics of every man in the colony. He was for a Church Establishment or he was against it. Blair's presence seemed to unite the "zealous Churchmen," to make them better acquainted with one another, and to prepare them for the second struggle for the Establishment which was now at hand.

Lord John Granville was the Palatine. He was a bigoted Churchman, and instructed Sir Nathaniel Johnson to see that the Church of England was made the Church of Carolina. The appointment of Johnson had been opposed by the Queen because she did not believe him well affected toward her succession to the crown. Johnson labored assiduously, therefore, to accomplish the desires of the Palatine.[2] He began with South Carolina. By dint of political trickery, some of it suggested by Lord Granville himself,[3] Johnson secured the passage of a law by the South Carolina Assembly, on May 6, 1704, which reproduced the essential principles of the Test Act of 1673.[4] It required all members of the Assembly to subscribe to the Act of 1678 which disabled the Papists; to take the oath of allegiance to Queen Anne; to receive the

[1] Col. Rec., I., 600 *et seq.* Efforts have been made by various writers, who base their arguments on this and similar instances, to show that there was in North Carolina " chronic objection to taxes in any form." But this " chronic objection " was by no means peculiar to North Carolina. " There is, in fact, reason to believe that one of the things against which our forefathers in England and the American colonies contended was not against oppressive taxation, but against the payment of any taxes at all." —Ely, Taxation in American States and Cities, p. 108.

[2] Hawks, II., 504 ; Caruthers, Life of David Caldwell, 60.

[3] Hawks, II., 505. *Cf.* also Col. Rec., I., 639, 640. The General Assembly was chosen with " very great partiality and injustice." " This act was passed in an illegal manner by the Governor's calling the Assembly to meet the 26th of April, when it then stood prorogued to the 10th of May following."

[4] For the terms of this Act, *cf.* p. 53, note 3.

sacrament according to the rites and usages of the Church
of England, or to swear and subscribe to an oath of conformity to the Church of England. A penalty of fifty pounds
for the first time the representative sat and ten pounds for
every day thereafter was inflicted on all who refused to conform to this act, because it "hath been found by experience
that the admitting of persons of different persuasions and
interests in matters of religion to sit and vote in the commons
house of Assembly, hath often caused great contentions and
animosities in this province, and hath very much obstructed
the public business."[1] On November 4 of the same year
the act was supplemented by a further act, consisting of
thirty-five sections, for "the Establishment of Religious
Worship in this Province according to the Church of England, and for the Erecting of Churches for the Public Worship of God, and also for the Maintenance of Ministers and
the Building Convenient Houses for them."[2] It established
a commission of twenty laymen, who were given the power,
on the request of nine parishioners and a majority of the
vestry, to cite the minister or rector before them, hear complaints against him, and if in their opinion the charges were
sustained, to remove him either by delivering such an
announcement into his hands, by leaving it at his home or by
fixing it to the church doors.[3]

Thus far all was well; but it seemed that a large part
of the inhabitants of South Carolina were not in sympathy
with the Church of England and were determined not to be
legislated into its folds. No mere act of human legislation
could mould the Dissenters of South Carolina, who were
composed of the same elements as the Dissenters in North
Carolina, into "one harmonious lump of piety and ortho-
doxy." The Dissenters drew up a petition in which their

[1] Act in Col. Rec. of North Carolina, II., 863–867.
[2] In Col. Rec., II., 867–882.
[3] Secs. xv. and xvi., Col. Rec., II., 873, 874. The acts were signed by
Granville, Carteret, Craven and Colleton. "Some of the Proprietors absolutely refused to join in the ratification of these acts." *Ibid.*, I., 635 *et seq.*

grievances were recited, and forwarded it to the Proprietors by
the hands of Joseph Boone.[1]   About the same time Edmund
Porter, a Quaker, appeared in England as the representative
of the complaints and grievances of the northern colony.[2]

Lord Granville, the Palatine, received the petition of his
subjects from the wilds of Carolina with haughty coldness.
It was pushed into the House of Lords. After hearing the
complaint of the colonists and the Proprietors through their
counsel, the Lords spiritual and temporal declared that the
law passed by the legislature of South Carolina for the
establishment of religious worship was "not warranted by
the charter granted to the Poprictors of that colony, as being
not consonant to reason, repugnant to reason, repugnant to
the laws of this realm, and destructive to the constitution of
the Church of England." They declared further that the act
requiring all members of the Assembly to take the oath,
subscribe to the declaration and conform in religious worship,
"is founded upon falsity in matter of fact, is repugnant to
the laws of England, contrary to the charter granted to the
Proprietors of that colony, is an encouragement to atheism and

---

[1] Petition in Col. Rec., I., 637 *et seq.*

[2] Martin, I., 219; Caruthers' Caldwell, 60; Hawks, II., 508. Dr. Hawks
says that Porter accompanied John Ash, who was sent to England from
South Carolina in 1703 to complain of the undue election of an Assembly,
of heavy taxes and impositions on trade (Col. Rec., II., 901 *et seq.*) ; but
this could not have been the case. The complaints which Ash carried are
dated June 26, 1703, and his published account of his mission was issued
in the same year. This was before the death of Walker, and consequently
there had been at that time no fresh disturbances in North Carolina. I
have been able to find no contemporary authority for the statement that
Edmund Porter was the man who went to England on this occasion, but
that such a messenger was sent there can be no doubt.   Missionary
Gordon, writing in 1709, says that about 1704 "the Quakers *sent complaints* against Colonel Daniel."   "In the year 1706 they sent one Mr.
John Porter to England, *with fresh grievances and new complaints.*"
(Col. Rec., I., 709.) This view is sustained by De Foe's "Party-Tyranny;
or, An Occasional Bill in Miniature ; As now Practiced in Carolina."
London, 1705 ; reprinted in Col. Rec., II., 891 *et seq.* It is not improbable
that Edmund Porter went over with Boone.

irreligion, is destructive to trade, and tends to the depopulating and ruining the said province."[1] This was not all. On the tenth of June, 1706, the obnoxious laws were repealed by proclamation of the Queen, and the Attorney-General was ordered to proceed against the Proprietors *in quo warranto* for a forfeiture of their charter.[2] Such were the opinions of the House of Lords and such the action of the Queen concerning the efforts to establish the Church of England in South Carolina.

While Daniel was Deputy Governor of North Carolina, late in 1704 or early in 1705, a law known as the " Vestry Act" was passed by the North Carolina Assembly, by "one or two votes." No copy of the act has been preserved, but Missionary Gordon says it provided that twelve vestrymen be chosen in each precinct; they had power to build a church in each and raise money from the inhabitants for that purpose; thirty pounds was provided for the minister whom the vestry by the act had power not only to disapprove but even to displace.[3] It has been said that this act was nothing more than a re-enactment of the Vestry Act of 1701, and its provisions as recorded by Gordon seem to sustain this hypothesis. It has been denied that it was as oppressive as the act passed about the same time by the South Carolina Assembly. It is said that the North Carolina act established a Church by law but did not require comformity thereto, and it is urged against the existence of such an act in North Carolina that we find no mention of North Carolina in the petition of the South Carolina Dissenters nor in the answer to their petition,[4] but have we a right to expect such a reference ? The South Carolinians were complaining of their own grievances and not of those of their northern neighbors and kinsmen; their petition was drawn up and signed in South Carolina, and because of the poverty of intercourse they may never have heard of the North Carolina

---

[1] Col. Rec., I., 636, 637.   [2] *Ibid.*, I., 642, 643.
[3] *Ibid.*, I., 709.   [4] *Ibid.*, I., Prefatory Notes, xxv. *et seq.*

troubles. The Dissenters in North Carolina, however, recognized the intimate connection between the two, and sent one
of their number three thousand miles to assist the representative from South Carolina in his mission. We cannot explain
why they would have been willing to incur such expense and
trouble had they not been vitally interested in the question
at issue. The Dissenters in North Carolina knew well
enough that if they could help the Dissenters in South
Carolina to a victory over the Churchmen there, then the dis-
tasteful laws passed by their own Assembly must also fall, and
hence there was neither cause nor reason for mentioning the
grievances under which they were themselves laboring. It is
unfortunate that the act has not been preserved among our
early laws, so that the question might be settled entirely;
but its absence means nothing whatever, for our records are
notoriously imperfect. The act is unmentioned by the
missionaries probably because there were no missionaries
in the province while it was in force, and those who came
later naturally felt a delicacy in bringing a matter into the
public gaze in which they and their interests had suffered a
most lamentable defeat, and a defeat coming, moreover, not
from their natural opponents, the Dissenters, but from the
highest authority in England, an authority disposed to sustain them under all reasonable circumstances. More than this,
the Assembly which passed the ecclesiastical laws of which
the Dissenters are now complaining had been secured only
"after many attempts," and no doubt by "a great deal of care
and management," as had the Assembly of 1701. The Dissenters had been thrown off their guard. We are told that the
law was passed by only "one or two votes," and that after
its passage the "Quakers, who, being still powerful in the
Council, numerous in the Assembly, and restless in their
endeavors, spared neither pains nor expense to have this act
repealed or altered."[1] Further, in regard to the act of 1701,

---

[1] Col. Rec., I., 709. This quotation does not refer to the act of 1701,
for it is not probable that Henderson Walker when writing to the Bishop

the Quakers simply collected their forces, elected a majority
of the members of the Assembly from their ranks, and
announced themselves as prepared to repeal the obnoxious
law at the next session of the Assembly. If the act of 1704
was not different from that of 1701, why is it treated so much
more seriously by the Dissenters? Why incur the expense
of an agent in England if their trouble was similar to that
in 1701? The fact that an agent was considered necessary
to attend to their interests indicates that the new law in
North Carolina was closely akin to that in South Carolina.

These certainly are the views which have been held by the
historians of the State. Martin says of Daniel, "This gentleman had it in charge to procure the establishment of the
Church of England by legal authority. The bill received
great opposition, but the address of the Governor secured its
passage. The act provided, among other things, for a fine on
any person holding a place of trust who should neglect to
qualify himself, by taking the oath required by law."[1]
Wheeler[2] says that "in 1704, by arts and intrigues in the
General Assembly, a law was passed by a majority of one,
disfranchising all Dissenters from any office of trust, honor,
or profit." Dr. Hawks,[3] quoting documents now not to be
had, says that "most prominent" in Daniel's instructions
"was the direction that he should kindle the torch of discord,
and destroy the brief repose to which Walker had happily
brought the province, by causing the Legislature of Albe-

---

of London would have left unmentioned so objectionable a clause as that
which placed the clergy under the control of the vestry, had it been in
the act of 1701. William Glover characterizes this clause as "a great
error," and when found in the South Carolina act, the House of Lords
said it was "destructive to the constitution of the Church of England."

[1] This quotation is from Martin, I., 222. The statements made may be
entirely wrong, but it is self-evident that Martin believed that the South
Carolina acts of 1704 were passed in North Carolina also. He mentions an
oath required of all persons holding "*a place of trust.*" In the North
Carolina vestry act of 1715 oaths are required of no one except the vestrymen.

[2] History, I., 34.   [3] II., 506.

marle to establish by law the Church of England in the northern part of Carolina."

From all the evidence we have on the subject, the writer is compelled to believe that the trouble was much more serious than it had been in 1701; that the North Carolina act was almost, if not entirely identical with the South Carolina acts of 1704. The evidence seems to indicate that men were required to conform to the English Church. We shall return to this phase of the question in discussing the causes of the "Cary rebellion"; but whether the Church Acts of North and South Carolina are identical or not is immaterial for the purposes of this paper. No one denies that an act was passed at this time which fixed an Established Church on the colony, and Dissenters were required to pay to its support. This was in itself insolence and intolerance, a retrogression from that state of practical religious freedom which the colonists had enjoyed prior to 1701, and a still further departure from the Protestant theory that every man carries within his own bosom the seat of authority, that each one is his own pope, and that none shall dare molest or make him afraid.

We now come to the so-called " Cary Rebellion," which is one of the most interesting, but at the same time one of the most involved events in our early history. In the troublesome times which followed Edmund Porter's mission to England, politics and religion are mixed together in almost inextricable confusion, and unfortunately all our materials come from the most bigoted and prejudiced of partisans. We must exercise the greatest care, then, in forming an estimate of the parties to this struggle from the evidence furnished us by the aristo-cratic party. Prominent among these witnesses is Thomas Pollock, the sworn foe of Edward Moseley, one of the popular leaders; another is Alexander Spotswood, Governor of Virginia, who, always notoriously unjust when writing of North Carolina affairs, could now pour out the vials of his wrath on the Dissenters, for he hated " a rebel only less than a Quaker, and a Quaker only less than the Father of Evil."[1] Edward Hyde, the successor to the claims of Glover, also adds condemnation to the Quakers, and Gordon the missionary, like all the Churchmen, found only evil in their lives, motives and principles.

The main outline of events as given by Gordon seems to be as follows. About the time the troubles caused by the Church Act of 1704 were at their height, an act passed in the first year of Queen Anne, requiring an oath of allegiance to her and her heirs in the Protestant line, reached North Carolina. Daniel presented this oath to the Quakers, who refused, it is said, to take it because they swore not at all. They were thereupon dismissed from the Council, the Assembly and courts of justice; moreover, a law was made that no one should hold any office or place of trust without taking these oaths.[2] To complain against this new regulation seems to have been one of the duties of Edmund Porter. It is probable also that the declaration of the House of Lords in regard to the religious acts in South Carolina was not without its good effect, for we find that the Proprietors, through the influence of Archdale,[1] who was opposed to this system of legislating religion into the colony, were prevailed on to remove Daniel from his overlordship in North Carolina and to appoint another deputy governor in his place.

This was done in 1705,[3] and Thomas Cary was nominated as the successor of Daniel. Cary had been a collector of quit-rents for the Proprietors.[4] He is perhaps the same as the Mr. Thomas Cary, a Carolina merchant, whom we meet on an earlier page of the records.[5] He, like John Culpepper, had been the leader in a popular uprising in South Carolina before coming to North Carolina.[6] He had possibly fled thence to

---

[1] Davis, A Study in Colonial History, p. 20.

[2] Col. Rec., I., 709. *Cf.* also Hawks, II., 509.

[3] Col. Rec., I., 709; Hawks, II., 440, 508.

[4] Williamson, I., 170. *Cf.* also Col. Rec., I., 723, 725.

[5] Col. Rec., I., 557.

[6] *Ibid.*, I., 801.

escape what he was soon to meet in his new home, and it is perhaps from this movement that he acquired his title of "colonel." His appointment seems to have given satisfaction at first to the Dissenters generally. When he came into power the Quakers made fresh efforts to obtain offices and a majority of the seats in the Assembly;[1] but Cary, like Daniel, tendered them the oaths of allegiance, which they again refused to take, and were again dismissed from the Council, the Assembly and the courts of justice. Cary procured, moreover, the enactment of a law by which any party who procured his own election or who sat and acted officially under any election without first taking the required oaths should forfeit five pounds for each offense.[2]

This law exasperated the Quakers and their allies, whom we may call the popular party. It seemed now that all their struggles for liberty were to become of no account, and that they were to be disfranchised by the man whose nomination they had sanctioned. They had wasted time and incurred expense in the struggle, and victory was too near in sight to be given up without another effort. In 1706 they sent John Porter as an agent to England, "with fresh grievances and new complaints."[3] Porter sympathized with but probably was not a member of the Society of Friends. He had married the daughter of Alexander Lillington; he was a man of prominence and influence and became the ancestor of a large and distinguished family.[4] He was successful in his efforts with the Proprietors. The authority of Governor Johnson was suspended; Cary was removed; several of the old deputies of the Proprietors were turned out of office; new appointments were made, and the power was given these deputies, who formed the council of the chief magistrate, to choose a new president of the Council from among themselves and he was to act as Governor.[1] Porter returned to North

---

[1] Col. Rec., I., 709.
[2] *Ibid.*, I., 709 ; Hawks, II., 509.
[3] Col. Rec., I., 709 *et seq.*
[4] Davis, 16 ; Ashe, A Chapter of North Carolina History Revised, 3.

Carolina in October, 1707, and from his return the "Cary Rebellion" may be said to date.

An effort has been recently made to explain the troubles which were now ready to culminate in the so-called "Cary Rebellion" as due solely to the refusal of the Quakers to take the oath of allegiance to Queen Anne, and not to any efforts to fix an Established Church in the colony.[1] If this is the true and only cause for the disturbance culminating in the deposition of Daniel from the deputy governorship in 1705 and of Cary in 1707, both under the authority and by the commands of the Lords Proprietors, we are put to the necessity of explaining how the Quakers, who were always numerically in the minority and who represented neither the wealth nor the intelligence of the colony,[2] were still able to retain the support of the other dissenting elements among the people, although the latter had no objection to taking the oath of allegiance, and, if we are to believe most accounts, were entirely too fond of swearing anyhow and practiced it on the slightest provocation. Nor will this theory explain the attachment of such men as Edward Moseley to the cause of the popular party. He had no objections to the oath; he was, moreover, a Churchman, and was therefore not in sympathy with the Quakers. It can be explained only when we remember that he was the broadest-minded man who lived in North Carolina during the first half of the eighteenth

---

[1] Col. Rec., I., Prefatory Notes, xxv. *et seq. Cf.* also Sketches of Church History in North Carolina, 54 *et seq.*, where the same position is taken.

[2] Missionary Gordon, writing in 1709, says that they were "very numerous" in Perquimans (Col. Rec., I., 713) and in Pasquotank (714) precincts. We learn from Rev. James Adams that this expression meant for Pasquotank 210 Quakers out of 1332 inhabitants (720). In Currituck there was one Quaker in a population of 539 (722). In Chowan there were "no Quakers or any other Dissenters" (712). In the letter just quoted Gordon says the Quakers were "but about the tenth part" of the inhabitants (711), and Adams says they were "not the seventh part" .(686). Gordon says that they were not wealthy, "there being but few or no traders of note amongst them," and they were not the real leaders in the colony, for "their ignorance and obstinacy are but too remarkable upon all occasions" (711).

century. He was a patriot rather than a partisan, and as such espoused the cause of religious freedom against the bigotry and narrowness of his age and country.

The fundamental idea in the "Cary Rebellion" may have been in part with the Quakers opposition to the oaths of allegiance;[1] but it was with the large body of Dissenters living in the colony and who were not Quakers, and with a few choice spirits among the Churchmen themselves, none the less a sharp and emphatic protest against the arrogance, pride and attempted oppression of the Churchmen. This second element of the struggle is a necessary corollary from the first when we ask ourselves the question, on what grounds, even with the assistance of Archdale, did the two Porters secure from the Proprietors the removal of Daniel, and later of Cary, apparently for the same reasons? One school of critics will have us believe that these men were removed from office simply because they performed a plain and simple duty required of them and of all other Governors by the Crown. If this is true, if the Proprietors removed their subordinates because these subordinates administered the oath of allegiance, which oath was required both by the common law and by the statute law of the realm, and which requirement the Queen had not and the Proprietors could not dispense with, would not the Proprietors in that case have been guilty of treason against the Crown? This point is virtually admitted by William Glover himself in his protest.[2] Was there not, beyond and beside this oath of allegiance, another and more offensive matter, as Mr. Moore says in his history of the State,[3] a test oath? The

---

[1] This view is not sustained by later events, however. When George I. came to the throne in 1714 he was proclaimed in North Carolina and the oath of allegiance was taken (Col. Rec., II., 146). The Quakers were as numerous and powerful as in 1704-5, but we find none of that uproar and confusion. When George II. succeeded, the most careful provisions were made in regard to the oaths of allegiance (*Ibid.*, III., 68, 69, 91, 109), but there was no rebellion on account of these oaths.

[2] Col. Rec., I., 698.

[3] I., 32. In March, 1673, a Test Act was passed by the British Parliament which compelled all persons holding office under the government to

spirit of the colonial charters was opposed to the discrimina-
tions rigidly enforced in England against Dissenters. No
officer in all England could escape subscribing to the Test
Act, but it was a dead letter in America; and had this not
been the case, Archdale could never have been Governor-
General of Carolina. This suspension of the law in favor
of the colonies was due largely to William III., who desired
complete religious toleration, if not equality among Protes-
tants.

The whole struggle seems to have been a repetition of that
of 1677, only transferred to another field. In 1677 the
trouble arose from the presence of a Governor who undertook
to enforce the Navigation Acts, which up to that time had
been a dead letter. In 1705 a Governor undertakes to enforce
the Test Act, which had been a dead letter hitherto, with the
ultimate hope of securing an Established Church. The result was rebellion. Some such view is absolutely necessary
to explain the extent of the dissatisfaction. The claim that
the Quakers, when the only plank in their platform was no
oaths of allegiance for the oath's sake, could have been able
to rally around their standard the majority of the inhabitants
of a province who favored the cause for which the oaths of
allegiance were created and who had no objections to swearing in itself, will not bear critical examination. The theory
of the oaths of allegiance as the main motive is enough to
explain neither the removal of Daniel nor of Cary, nor the
wide extent of the revolt.

Having examined the causes leading up to the " rebellion," we are now prepared to retrace our steps and resume
the narrative of events ; and only when the actions of the
popular party are viewed in the light of the troubles do they

---

take the oath of allegiance and supremacy, to abjure transubstantiation,
and to take the sacrament according to the Established Church. This act
together with the Corporation Act was repealed in May, 1828, through
the efforts of Lord John Russell. A declaration containing the words "on
the true faith of a Christian " was substituted for the sacramental test,
thus admitting Protestant Dissenters to office.

become at all comprehensible as the actions of reasonable
and thinking men.

After Porter returned from England and announced the
instructions which he had received from the Proprietors, a
day was appointed on which the old officers were to be suspended and the new ones to be qualified;[1] but before that day
arrived Porter called the new deputies together, a majority
of whom were Quakers, and had them choose William Glover
as President of the Council. He thus became Governor of
the province *ex-officio*, and Cary was suspended as Daniel
had been.[2]

Glover was a resident of Perquimans and had been a
clerk of the court in that precinct in 1699.[3] Three years
later he had become a justice of the supreme court of the
colony.[4] He was a Churchman, but the popular party seem
to have thought him favorable to their interests, and his
election was sanctioned by Col. Cary, Porter and other
leaders.[5] It was believed that the hateful laws against
which they had been struggling, *whatever the nature of these
laws may have been,* would now be regarded as a dead letter,
since the action of the Proprietors in removing Daniel and
Cary, who had both undertaken to enforce them, was the
plainest and most direct evidence that these laws were not
intended for the province. It was not to be supposed that
the Governors of the province would undertake to do more
than was required of them by the Proprietors, or what was
directly against the will of the Proprietors, as the enforcement of the hateful acts and oaths was. Whatever may
have been the legal relations of the popular party to the
Proprietors hitherto, they now appear not as rebels hinder-
ing the course of law, but as patriots defending the rights
granted them by the Proprietors and the English government; while their opponents could no longer pose as the
representatives of law and order, but had clearly become

---

[1] Col. Rec., I., 710.   [2] *Ibid.*, I., 709 *et seq.*
[3] *Ibid.*, I., 522.   [4] *Ibid.*, I., 566.   [5] *Ibid.*, I., 727.

usurpers, tyrants and autocrats, as far as they were able.
Matters were precipitated, moreover, in April, 1708, by the
arrival of Gordon and Adams, the new missionaries of the
Society for the Propagation of the Gospel. The Establishment threatened to become more oppressive than ever, and it
is no wonder that when Glover, like Daniel and Cary, tendered the popular party the ever present and ever hateful
oaths, they, with their leader Porter, turned against him.
Porter gets the old and the new deputies together, reverses
the election of Glover, strikes up a friendship with Cary,
who had perhaps promised to accede to their demands, and
gets him chosen President of the Council and therefore
ex-officio Governor, and all this by virtue of the very commission that had removed him from office.[1]

Just as was to be expected, Glover and his party refused
to recognize Cary as Governor; but the popular party did
not cease their efforts, and the result was that the colony
enjoyed for a while the tender mercies of rival governments.
In this struggle the popular party is not so clearly in the
wrong as some historians of the State, most notably Dr.
Hawks,[2] would have us believe. He says that Cary's second
election was accomplished by men who were unqualified for
the duty, the old deputies having been suspended and the
new ones unsworn; but Dr. Hawks forgets that Glover had
been elected by the new deputies before they had been
sworn; his election was therefore illegal and void and Cary
was still Governor *de jure.* The truth is that John Porter
was the cleverest politician in all colonial North Carolina.
He outwitted the Church party so completely on this occasion
that its defenders are still unable to comprehend his policy.
The pretended election of Glover was simply intended by
the astute politician as a feeler to indicate the true position
of the two aspirants for gubernatorial honors toward the
great question of the day, the test oaths. No one knew

---

[1] Col. Rec., I., 709 *et seq.*
[2] History, II., 510.

better than Porter that under the circumstances the election of Glover was null and void. He soon discovered that Glover was not the friend of the popular party. Cary probably promised to respect their wishes if allowed to retain his office ; this promise was accepted and the last instructions of the Proprietors were ignored.

Some such interpretation as this is necessary to explain the success of the popular party. To say, as Dr. Hawks and Mr. Moore have said, that Glover was deposed, Cary re-elected and supported for three years simply to gratify the *personal spite* of Porter, is to charge the colonists with a cowardly submission to one-man power which they never showed on other occasions, even if that power was exercised by an appointee of the Proprietors or by a Proprietor himself. The question at issue was one of principle, not one of personal likes and dislikes.

The double government continued during 1708. In order to settle the troubles it was resolved to refer the rival claims to the Assembly for decision. Both Cary and Glover issued writs for the election. The Assembly met October 11, 1708, at the house of Capt. John Hacklefield on Little river in Perquimans county. It had twenty-six members; of these five were sent from each of the four precincts of Albemarle county and two from each of the three precincts of Bath county. Pasquotank and Perquimans precincts sent Cary delegates and so did Bath county, " whose interest it was to stand by Col. Cary, for fear of being called to account for that seditious petition."[1] The popular party had therefore a majority in the Assembly, but, like political parties of to-day, proceeded to further strengthen themselves by seating Cary delegates from Chowan, where Glover delegates had received a majority of the votes cast and had been duly elected. The Assembly organized by electing Edward Moseley speaker. He was now first coming to the front in the political arena, and for the next forty years was destined to play no unimportant

---

[1] Col. Rec., I., 697 *et seq.*

part in the affairs of the colony. He was a Churchman, but
espoused the cause of the popular party with all the ardor of
his nature, and throughout all the trying struggle appears as
a man far above the level of his surroundings, as one who
was able to put aside matters that were personally preferable
and temporarily advantageous, for the sake of the good that
was to finally come from a broader and more statesmanlike
policy. The Lower House was now ready for business. The
Upper House was double, for Cary and his council sat in
one room, Glover and his council sat in another, while Col.
Daniel, who was a landgrave and therefore entitled to a seat
in the Upper House, sat first with one claimant and then with
the other.[1] The democratic Lower House proceeded to pass
an act nullifying the test oaths, and cut the gordian knot by
recognizing Cary as President and hence *ex-officio* Governor.
Glover protested. He offered to prove (1) that he was law-
fully the President of the Council, to him and to no other
belonged the execution of the Lords Proprietors' commission;
(2) that Cary was not President of the Council and had no
lawful power in North Carolina; (3) that if he were to die
or were to be removed by the Proprietors, Cary was not qualified to be elected or to exercise the powers of the President.
To this protest the Lower House replied curtly that they
would not concern themselves with this matter.[1] It is said
that both sides appealed to arms. Gordon, the missionary,
even tells us that one man had been killed before he left the
colony, and therefore before the meeting of the Assembly;
but there is very slight evidence to show that there was anything like civil war in the colony at this time. But for a time
there was, no doubt, anarchy and confusion. Old John Urmstone, the rum-soaked missionary, says, "for two years and
upwards here was no law, no justice, Assembly or courts of
judicature, so that people did and said what they list";[2] but
this is only a characteristic outburst of the missionary and is
harmless from the historical point of view. The internal

---

[1] Col. Rec., I., 697 *et seq.*   [2] *Ibid.*, I., 768.

evidence of the Records indicates that peace was to a great
extent restored and that the Proprietors recognized the government of Cary; but the popular party made use of their
power to persecute their opponents.   Some of these, among
them Glover, and Thomas Pollock, his staunchest supporter,
found it expedient to remove to the neighboring confines of
Virginia, as they were altogether too patriotic to live under a
government which they knew to be "altogether illegal."[1]

The arrival of Edward Hyde in North Carolina during
the summer of 1710[2] promised to settle the matters in dispute, but at the cost of restoring the Church party to power
and reëstablishing the Church of England.   Hyde had been
sent out by Col. Edward Tynte, then Governor-General of
Carolina; but owing to the death of Tynte he had no commission and could get none.   Private letters in his possession went to substantiate his claims, however, and it seems
that all parties being anxious to bring their internal quarrels
to an end and to restore harmony on all sides, united in a
petition to him to assume the duties of President of the
Council until his commission should arrive.[3]   Hyde assumed
the duties of President late in 1710.   In July of the next
year the Proprietors recommended that he be made "Governor of the North Part of Carolina."   By virtue of the commission which followed this recommendation Hyde became
in name the first Governor of North Carolina.[4]   .

Soon after becoming President, Hyde issued writs for an
Assembly.   It met in March, 1711.[5]   The Church party was
now again in power, and the opportunity for vengeance thus
given them was more than they could resist.   They proceeded to pass acts " wherein," remarks Gov. Spotswood,
"it must be confessed they showed more their resentment of
their ill usage during Mr. Cary's usurpation (as they call it)
than their prudence to reconcile the distractions of the coun-

---

[1] Col. Rec., I., 731.   [2] *Ibid.*, I., 731, 737, 779.
[3] *Ibid.*, I., 780, 785.   [4] *Ibid.*, I., 775.   [5] *Ibid.*, I., 806.

try,"[1] and to make such laws as not even the Proprietors could approve. They enacted a sedition law by which all persons guilty of "seditious words or speeches" or "scurrilous libels" against the then existing government were to be punished by "fine, imprisonment, pillory or otherwise at the discretion of the justices of the general court." The criminal was furthermore required to give security for good behavior "during the court's pleasure," and to be incapable of holding any place of trust for three years.[2] The act aimed a direct blow at the Quakers by providing a fine of £100 on all officers who refused to qualify themselves "according to the strictness of the laws in Great Britain now in force."[2] It also provided that "all such laws made for the establishment of the Church" as well as the laws "granting indulgences to Protestant dissenters . . . are and shall be in force." In another act it was provided that Col. Cary should be compelled to give an account of the funds then in his hands belonging to the Proprietors and which he had refused to pay out for the subsistence of the Palatines according to their order; that Edward Moseley should give security in the sum of £500 for the repayment of fees said to have been illegally extorted by him; and lastly, all suits, judgments, proceedings and levies made between July 24, 1708—the time of the second election of Cary—and January 22, 1711, were declared null and void.[3]

Besides passing a Sedition Act, bringing Cary and Moseley into custody for alleged misappropriation of funds, and disfranchising the Quakers through the requirements of the Test Act, this Assembly undertook to promote the cause of religion and morality by passing an act for the establishment of the Church. The act itself has not come down to us, but its provisions have been preserved in a letter of John Urmstone to the Society for the Propagation of the Gospel on the 7th of

[1] Col. Rec., I., 780.
[2] *Ibid.*, I., 787 *et seq.*, where the act is given.
[3] *Ibid.*, I., 791 *et seq.*

July, 1711, in which he says: "I . . . did all I could both in public and private discourse to excite them to use their endeavors to establish the Church ; accordingly they made a very good and proper act to that end, which was to this effect, that the worship of God and our most holy religion as by law established in England should be put in practice and observed here in all particulars as far forth as is compatible with the circumstances of the people. A select vestry of twelve men in every precinct or parish was thereby appointed ; all the Burgesses were made members thereof. These bound in a penalty to meet in their several parishes on a certain day within six weeks after the publication of the act to choose . churchwardens, give them power to buy a glebe, build a church or churches, as there was occasion houses for ministers, provide a sufficient maintenance for them, and to use their utmost to provide that every parish might be supplied with a clergyman, approved of, allowed, by the Lord Bishop of London."[1] We shall see that these laws caused more trouble immediately.

Matters had been in a fair way for settlement just after the coming of Hyde, for "his great candor and graceful behavior so far prevailed with the best and the awful respect to his family and interests" so overawed others that Col. Cary found himself almost deserted[2] and himself joined in the common petition to Hyde to assume the government.[3] But the malignity and severity of the new laws aroused the people ; Cary again found himself at the head of the popular party and determined to resist the execution of the laws. He so fortified his house " with guns and other warlike stores " that "when the government had taken a resolution to apprehend him they found it impracticable."[3] He became aggressive ; he fitted out a brigantine of six guns and went to attack Hyde and his Council, threatening to reënact in North Carolina the bloody scenes recently witnessed in Antigua,[4] where

[1] Col. Rec., I., 769.   [2] *Ibid.*, I., 785.
[3] *Ibid.*, I., 780.   [4] *Ibid.*, I., 782, 795.

Governor Parke, who had acted as a ruthless tyrant for three years, was torn in pieces by an infuriated mob and fed to wild beasts. Such a threat did not create a very pleasing impression in the gubernatorial circles of North Carolina and Virginia, and Governor Spotswood offered his mediation.[1] Each side seemed afraid of the other; hostilities continued, and on June 30, Cary, unterrified by any "awful reverence" of family, attempted to capture Governor Hyde.[2] Spotswood thereupon interfered in behalf of the established government. He sent a body of marines to the scene of disturbance, and the presence of English troops "frightened the rebellious party so as to lay down their arms and disperse."[3]

Thus ended the "Cary rebellion," July, 1711. Some of the leaders fled to Virginia, where a proclamation was issued ordering that Thomas Cary, John Porter, Edmund Porter, Emanuel Lowe and Nevil Lowe his son, Richard Roach and others be seized and held in a bond of £500 each.[4] Thomas Cary, Levi Truehit, Challingwood Ward, George Lumley, Edmund Porter were seized in Virginia and hurried off to England before the authorities in North Carolina had had time to collect their evidence.[5] This evidence does not seem to have been forwarded, and in May, 1713, Col. Cary again arrived in North Carolina.[6] In the same year the government received curt instructions from the Queen to send no more prisoners to England for trial "without good proof first made of their crimes and that proof transmitted along with the prisoner."[7] The government had already received instructions to suspend persecution against the popular party until a commissioner appointed to investigate the troubles should arrive from England,[8] and when this persecution ceased the troubles came to an end.

The evil effects of the "Cary rebellion" were many and long-continued. It had been an unsuccessful struggle against oppression in Church and State; the people when

---

[1] Col. Rec., I., 780.   [2] *Ibid.*, I., 782, 802.   [3] *Ibid.*, I., 800.
[4] *Ibid.*, I., 776.   [5] *Ibid.*, I., 806, 807.   [6] *Ibid.*, II., 46, 53.
[7] *Ibid.*, II., 63.   [8] *Ibid.*, II., 53.

they emerged from it were naturally stubborn and apathetic toward a government which did not have their confidence or respect and which in turn said that they were " unreasonable and ungovernable." The popular party had been beaten by the other side; they submitted, but with sullen stubbornness. For their part, the Churchmen found no terms too vile to apply to their opponents. They called them rebels, " Quakers, atheists and deists," [2] and all these terms seem to have been with them very nearly identical in meaning. They accused them of instigating the horrible Indian massacre of September, 1711. In regard to this unfortunate occurrence Gov. Spotswood says in his most insinuating way that Cary " threatened to bring down the Tuscarora Indians to his assistance," and that " Mr. Porter, one of Cary's pretended Council, was with the Tuscarora Indians endeavoring by promises of great rewards to engage them to cut off all the inhabitants of that part of Carolina that adhered to Mr. Hyde." [3] He says in another place that " several affidavits " had been sent to him to prove that Porter had promised the Indians " great rewards " to cut off Hyde's adherents.[4] The charge that the adherents of Cary incited the Tuscaroras is preposterous; there is no evidence to support the *ipse dixit* of the Church party. But while such a charge is contrary to reason, it has been accepted as the real motive of the Indian uprising by at least one historian of the State. Dr. Hawks has no love for the popular party in the " Cary rebellion," nor for its leaders. Here he has ceased to hold the position of the careful, critical, historical investigator and has chosen instead the sphere of an advocate. He was doubtless influenced to take this position by his excessive devotion to Pollock, the right-hand man of Glover, the champion of the Establishment and the steady opponent of the extension of popular liberty. The Tuscarora war followed the internal dissensions of the colony, *post hoc, ergo propter hoc.*

---

[1] Col. Rec., I., 881.   [2] Pollock to Hyde, *Ibid.*, I., 731.
[3] Col. Rec., I., 782 *et seq.*   [4] *Ibid.*, I., 796.

The true reason for the war is to be found in the steady encroachments of the whites on the lands of the Indians. These were being driven steadily westward; they saw that they must soon give up the hunting grounds of their fathers to the white man; they were irritated beyond measure; they saw that the colony was now weak and helpless through divisions, enmities and hostilities among themselves; they saw that the time had come for them to strike: the result was war. It was because they summarized in John Lawson, the historian and surveyor-general of the colony, all the evils which they had suffered that they put him to death. They mistook him for a cause, while he had been only an agent. That they were not instigated to their attack by any faction is shown by the absolute impartiality with which they slaughtered all settlers exposed to them. The Palatines at New Bern suffered heavily although they had taken no part in the Cary troubles and had arrived after these troubles had been partly settled. The people of Bath county had been attached to the cause of Col. Cary, as we have seen, but still they were among the heaviest sufferers. Is it reasonable to suppose that even the "Quakers, atheists and deists" of North Carolina would have incited the savages to murder their own followers? The outlying settlements along the Neuse and Roanoke suffered heavily. These were composed largely of members of the Church party, but the inhabitants in Chowan did not suffer although some of the Tuscaroras were living in Bertie and had all opportunities for attacking them. Nor were the Churchmen troubled in Currituck, although there were Indians in that section who might have been "excited." The fact that the savages spared neither age nor sex and made all their attacks on outlying settlements regardless of the side the settlers took in the politics of the day, must forever belie the claims of Spotswood and his followers that they were instigated to the slaughter by Cary and his partisans.

In a subsequent paper the writer hopes to continue his account of the growth of the Established and of the Dissenting churches.   He will show that in 1730 the government undertook to enforce in North Carolina the atrocious Schism Act, which had been repealed in England as early as 1718 ; that Dissenting clergymen were denied for years the privilege of performing the marriage ceremony ; that this was finally granted them only under burdensome restrictions, and that during the whole of the colonial period the Dissenting population was steadily exploited in favor of the Establishment.   He will also trace the development of that spirit of opposition to an Establishment which was to culminate in the Declaration of Rights and in the State Constitution of 1776, in the first amendment to the Federal Constitution in 1789, and in the final triumph of absolute religious freedom by the removal in 1835 of the ban placed on Roman Catholics by the State Constitution in 1776.

SOURCES OF INFORMATION ON THE RELIGIOUS DEVELOPMENT IN NORTH CAROLINA.

The chief source of information for the colonial history of North Carolina is the Colonial Records of North Carolina, (10 volumes, quarto, Raleigh, 1886–1890), edited by Hon. William L. Saunders, Secretary of State for North Carolina, who brought to his work great love and a tireless energy. But while full on the political and social side, the Records are meagre on the religious side. Besides extracts from Edmundson and Fox there is nothing prior to 1701, when the minutes of the Vestry of St. Paul's Parish, Chowan precinct, and the minutes of the Friends' Monthly Meetings in Pasquotank precinct begin, the latter being, according to the editor, the earliest records of the Friends. This is an error. Manuscript records of Monthly Meetings going back to 1680 are now in possession of Josiah Nicholson, Esq., of Belvidere, Perquimans county, and were used in the preparation of this paper. Other manuscript records representing the work of the Yearly, Quarterly and Monthly Meetings, and going back almost to 1700, are now at Guilford College, North Carolina, but some of these were seriously damaged by the burning of one of the college buildings a few years ago. The parts of the journals of Edmundson and Fox relating to North Carolina are reprinted in Colonial Records, vol. I. Other Quaker missionaries visited the colony and their journals have been of service, as Thomas Chalkley (New York, 1808), James Dickenson (Philadelphia, 1848), Thomas Story (London, 1786), and Thomas Wilson (London, 1784). Later and excellent accounts of the growth and development of the Friends in North Carolina are to be found in Bowden's History of the Society of Friends in America (London, 1850) and in Janney's History of the Religious Society of Friends (Philadelphia, 1867).

In 1704 the voluminous correspondence of the missionaries of the S. P. G. begins, and is to be found in the Colonial Records. Dr. Charles Lee Smith, in his History of Education in North Carolina (Washington, 1888), has shown the value of these missionaries as school-teachers, and in the *Trinity (N. C.) Archive* for October, 1891, Dr. Stephen B. Weeks points out their work as the founders of the first public libraries.

The best short accounts of the settlement and growth of the colony of North Carolina, and the most reliable ones, are those by Bancroft (History U. S.) and by Prof. William J. Rivers in the Narrative and Critical History of America (Vol. V., Chap. V.). Caruthers, in his Life of David Caldwell (Greensboro, N. C., 1842), gives an account of church matters which is based on Martin. Rev. L. C. Vass, in his History of the Presbyterian Church in New Bern (Richmond, 1886), gives a *résumé* of early ecclesiastical affairs in Eastern North Carolina. The religious development is touched by the historians of the State in course. The fullest account is that of Dr. Hawks, who devotes a chapter to "Religion and Learning" (Vol. II., 291–370, Fayetteville, N. C., 1858), and reprints some original documents. But Dr. Hawks is a thorough Churchman; he has no sympathy for the Dissenters, and the popular party in the " Cary Rebellion " is handled very roughly. This part of his work, so far as it relates to Edward Moseley and John Porter, has been ably answered by Hon. George Davis in A Study in Colonial History (Wilmington (N. C.), 1880). Capt. Samuel A. Ashe, in A Chapter of North Carolina History Revised (*News and Observer*, December 31, 1886, and reprinted), defends the leaders in the "Cary Rebellion" against the aspersions of Dr. Hawks, but finds the chief trouble to have been the oath of allegiance.

In the *North Carolina University Magazine*, IX., p. 159 (1889–90), Hon. William H. Bailey discusses The State of Religion in the Province of North Carolina. The subject of religion is but scantily treated in the latest history of the State by Maj. John W. Moore (2 vols., Raleigh, 1880). The latest contribution to this field is Sketches of Church History in North Carolina, a series of papers read before the joint Convention of the Dioceses of North Carolina and East Carolina in Tarboro in 1890, which has just appeared.

www.ingramcontent.com/pod-product-compliance
Lightning Source LLC
Chambersburg PA
CBHW021514090426
42739CB00007B/610

* 9 7 8 3 3 3 7 1 3 0 8 4 8 *